THINKERS &TINKERS

We're on a mission to inspire children with modern stories to create a brighter future.

For more Thinkers & Tinkers books check out
www.thinkersandtinkers.org

ISBN: 979-8-9868950-0-0

"When something is important enough,
you do it even if the odds are not in your favor."

– Elon Musk

ELON MUSK
MAKING THE IMPOSSIBLE POSSIBLE

written by:

Jeffrey Ouyang & Keith Larsen

illustrated by:

Keith Larsen

Hi, _____. My name is Elon Musk!

I'm an inventor and entrepreneur.
I want to make the world a better place.

And I have a dream to use rockets to send people to other planets...

like **Mars**!

I wasn't always a successful inventor, though.
I had to learn how to make the *impossible possible!*

My life story may not be
too different from yours.

Let me show you what I mean.

When I was your age, I was one of the smallest kids at my school. I got bullied a lot!

The bullying got so bad that I often thought it would be impossible to get through school.

What really helped me was reading books.
Books taught me that the impossible was possible.

I could be whoever I wanted to be: an inventor,
an entrepreneur, or even a superhero!

Besides reading, I loved playing video games. I loved video games so much that I wanted to learn how to make them.

Everyone told me it would be impossible to learn.

But, when I got my first computer, I taught myself how to build a game by reading in just three days!

Soon, I created a space-themed game called Blastar,
which I sold to grown-ups for money!

I learned that it wasn't impossible to make video games.

Once I got older, I left where I was born in South Africa to go to school in Canada and The United States.

While I was at graduate school, I had my first big idea to make the world a better place.

So, I took a break to see if I could make my idea possible.

My big idea was to help people find local businesses in cities on the internet— like an online map!

Everyone told me my idea was impossible.

I started working on the idea with my brother, Kimbal. We called the company Zip2.

We lived and slept in the office, working all day and night.

The days were long and hard, but we always believed in our impossible idea.

After hundreds of hours of hard work,
we made the *impossible possible!*

ZIP2

We then sold the company because I had another
idea to make the world a better place.

My next idea was to make it easier for people to buy and sell things online using a computer.

Again, everyone told me my idea was impossible.

IMPOSSIBLE!

BANK

With a lot of hard work and by reading many books...

I made the *impossible possible* again!

I created my second company, PayPal,
which I later sold for a lot of money.

With all this money, I didn't want to sit around and do nothing.

I'm an inventor and entrepreneur. I want to help people and make the world a better place!

Remember those goals I told you at the beginning of this book?

My first goal is to make the world a healthier place.
That's why I joined an electric car company called Tesla.

We make cars that use electricity instead of gas because it's better for the planet and the air we breathe!

Everyone told me it was impossible to make electric cars better than gas cars. But I've learned that nothing is impossible!

After years of hard work, we introduced the models S, X, 3, and Y, which are now the most popular electric cars in the world.

They're all **100%** gas-free!

My next goal was to find a way for people to travel to other planets, so I started a company called SpaceX.

But there was one problem.

I didn't know how to build a rocket!

Everyone, of course, told me it was impossible.
So I did what I loved most.

$$\left(\frac{\Delta m}{\Delta t}\right)v$$

$$E = mc^2$$

$$\infty \qquad \pi$$

$$2 + 2 = 4$$

I started reading books to
learn how it could be done.

ROCKET
SCIENCE

IMPOSSIBLE!

After building our first rocket, we tried to launch it into space. But it **FAILED**.

We tried a second time. And that **FAILED**.

Then a third time, **FAILED**.

And we never gave up. Until...

on our fourth try, the rocket launched successfully!

And in 2017, the SpaceX team launched and landed CRS-13, the world's first reusable rocket.

We made the *impossible possible!*

We then launched a rocket called Falcon Heavy into space. We even put a Tesla car on it!

It's now traveling **193,150,000** miles toward Mars!

(one hundred ninety three million,
one hundred fifty thousand)

Many people will tell you what you want to do is impossible.

IT'S POSSIBLE!

But when you work hard and believe in yourself, you can make the *impossible* **POSSIBLE**.

You can make the world a better place!

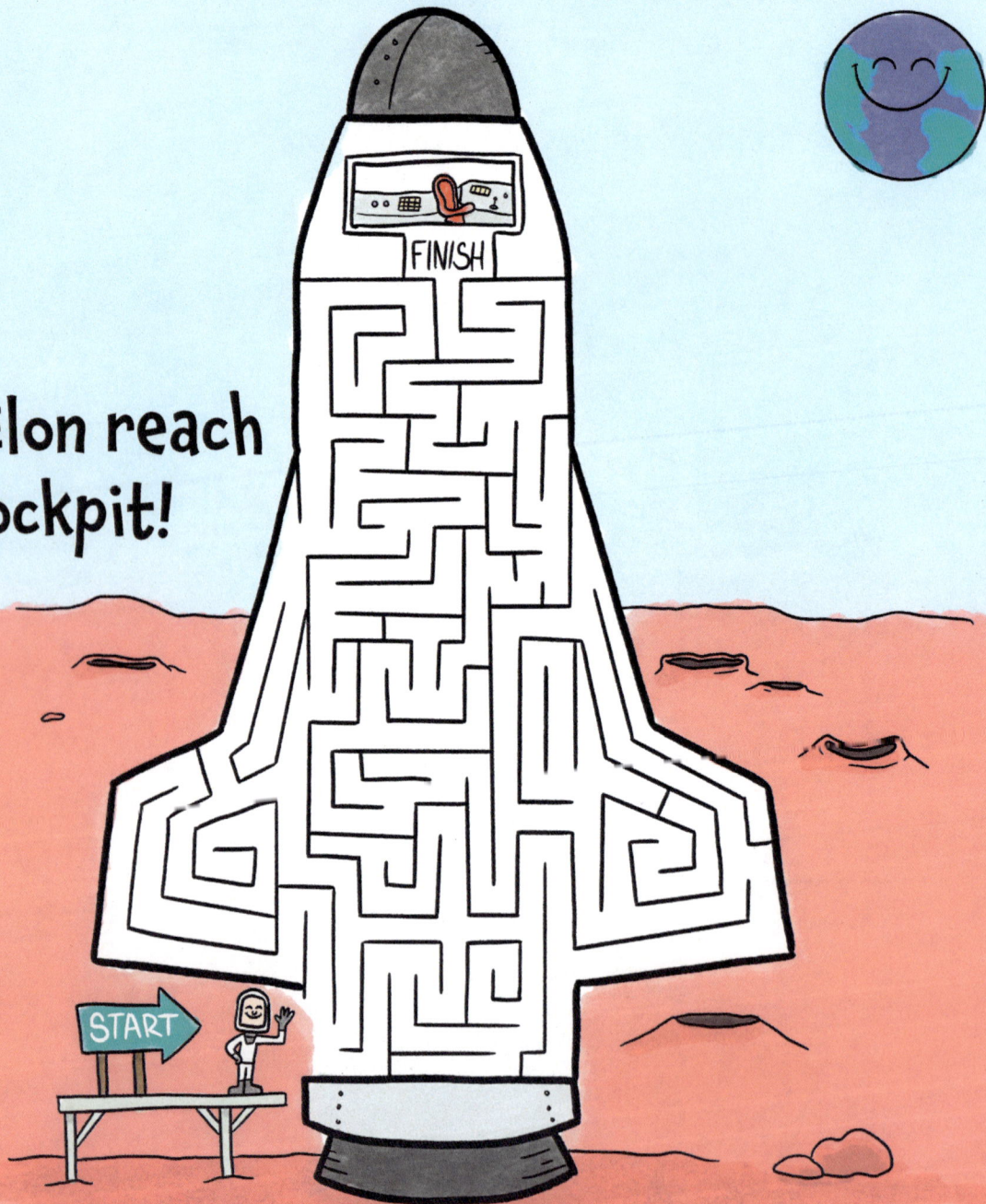
Help Elon reach the cockpit!

Elon's Word Search

Circle the words in the puzzle below

```
U A S O H N S R S
R P X T S T O D R
O C O T U T R S A
C B B S N U P A M
K X B E S A G T E
E Y V O C I V E U
T N O E O K B S Q
I N C K K K E L F
P L A N E T S A E
```

books   earth   inventor
mars   planet   possible
rocket   space   tesla

Made in the USA
Coppell, TX
12 March 2023